An Introduction to
Value Assurance

A Guide to Driving Effective Programs, Projects, Products, Services and Systems

Martyn R. Phillips

Certified Value Specialist
Professional Engineer

and

Shamsi B. Shishevan

Project Management Professional
Risk Management Professional

3rd Edition: November 2012;   Amended: June 2017

ISBN-10: 1480011959   ISBN-13: 978-1480011953

Contents: An Introduction to Value Assurance

Compiled by: Value Assurance Resources 360 Inc.
 Improving Program & Project Efficiencies

Further information may be obtained from: info@valueassurance.org

Originated in Canada

Preface

Expectations of performance and value can vary significantly with stakeholder purview and timing of consideration. The *Closing the Performance Gap* books series relates to portfolio, program and project leadership. This includes stakeholder consensus-building, collaborative working, innovation, setting clear and tested direction, along with ensuring accountability and effective change management for sustainable results.

Taking a look at programs and projects from a business management perspective:

❖ How do you demonstrate that your portfolios, programs and projects are providing best overall value for stakeholders?

❖ Is a critical program creeping over budget, behind schedule, out of scope or causing some concern to stakeholders?

❖ How effective is your planning, controls, reporting and approvals framework at ensuring efficient delivery of sustaining, competitive and effective business outcomes?

❖ How wide is the gap between your stakeholders' expectations and the performance / value that should be attainable?

❖ How are you managing the risk of not your stakeholders' expectations?

❖ Is there an explicit process for dealing with the important issue areas above?

The principles of *value assurance* (VA) apply to a wide range of portfolios, programs and projects. The VA process is ideal for identifying optimal concepts, driving out waste, building stakeholder consensus, improving timeframes, managing risk & value and responding to changing circumstances.

Figure A.   Portfolio, Program and Project Interrelationships

Preface (Continued)

The VA process creates powerful insights and steers undertakings toward better solutions in less time, with the optimal use of resources. It guides and ensures that developing solutions are appropriate and up-to-date for the needs. **VA is particularly useful for guiding business change initiatives, such as new systems to increase performance, as well as complex capital endeavors that will bring about significant or rapid change.**

Closing the *performance/value gap* successfully is not just a "quick fix", but it is attained through a continuous series of pre-emptive management actions that are conducted from end to end, i.e. throughout the life cycle –from the investment decision phase, through development and execution, to routine operation. Programs require alignment of expectations, robust project management and assurance of results.

The framework comprises a process for ensuring best overall value through value assurance for a) value identification, and b) value realization over the longer term. This is accomplished through the application of well-focused, strategic value planning, followed by performance monitoring and value enhancement. Typical outcomes include optimum functionality, life cycle cost, return-on-investment and schedule; plus managed risk and stakeholder consensus, along with systematic assurance of best overall value and performance.

See **Figure A** for an example of portfolio, program and project interrelationships. Note that some projects may be much larger than entire programs or portfolios elsewhere. Hence procedures must be appropriate to the situation. Managing for best value is a lifestyle that can be embedded into the culture of any organization.

This series of books (see page 39) covers a broad range of topics for application to undertakings of various sizes and complexity. Judicious selection of the many available tools and techniques should be made according to the situation in hand.

66 *Innovation keeps businesses competitive – it is*

widely recognized as providing a real impetus

for growth and is at the heart of corporate

strategy in many of the world's leading firms *99*

Source: Confederation of British Industry

Contents

Synopsis

Programs and projects that are driven and developed by "recipes", or by precedent, tend to lose an indeterminate amount of potential value for stakeholders. Such loss of value may be through unidentified opportunities, unnecessary risk, conflicts with other programs/projects, poor functionality, sub-optimal scheduling, disjointed coordination, excessive costs, inadequate return-on- investment and forfeited profitability.

Value assurance (VA) is an overarching, business and function-based management process. VA is applied for the entire duration of a program or major project from inception, through development and installation, to operation and final disposition. VA ensures balanced solutions and is applicable to both "hard" and "soft" types of endeavors.

Assurance for stakeholders is provided such that their portfolios, programs and projects remain viable in terms of:
- Business aims (benefits, R.O.I., scope and costs)
- User requirements (availability, serviceability, operability, reliability and compliance capabilities)
- Technical merit (feasibility and fitness-for-purpose)
- Supply chain capabilities and compatibilities
- Likelihood of meeting forecast targets
- In-service continuing effectiveness & financial efficiency.

VA provides an integrated approach to developing and controlling initiatives. It guides the setting of realistic targets and focuses on aspects that are most worthwhile, especially in terms of time, resources and return on investment. VA is also a navigational and decision-enabling aid that establishes strategic direction and optimizes use of corporate resources as well as maximizing performance gains, shareholder returns and wider stakeholder satisfaction.

VA affords a pro-active, holistic and systematic way of building stakeholder consensus and driving best value through an end-to-end program / project delivery, planning and assurance mechanism. The basic premise of value assurance is illustrated in **Figure B**.

Level:

Executive
- *Portfolio &*
Program
Oversight

VALUE ASSURANCE

Ensure BEST VALUE for the
Taxpayer, Shareholder, etc.

 Higher
Order
Function

PERFORMANCE ASSESSMENT & REPORTING

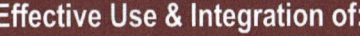

WHY

Management
- *Coordination*
of Performance
Assurance & Value
Improvement
Program(s)

Develop High Performance
Organization, Portfolio,
Programs and Projects

HOW

VALUE METHODOLOGY / MANAGEMENT

Practitioner
- *Application of*
Value Methodology,
Risk Management
and Other
Related
Techniques

Effective Use & Integration of:
➢ Strategic Direction
➢ Consultation
➢ Issues Management
➢ Systems & Procedures
➢ Tools & Resources
➢ Team Building

Figure B. Premise for Value Assurance

A high performance portfolio is obtained through a variety of methods, tools and techniques. High performance is required to maximize value for taxpayers, shareholders and other stakeholders. There are three levels to consider: 1. executive oversight (value assurance); 2. coordination of performance reviews, enhancements and overview reporting; 3. value & risk management interventions.

Value also tends to be eroded over time. VA is accomplished through holistic, longer-term thinking and application of a suite of universal and interconnected "best practices". The essence of this approach is a continuum of participatory strategic planning, group problem-solving and the explicit management of risk and value; - along with effective change management and a system of linked, multi-level performance reporting and course correction.

Figure C illustrates the application areas for a continuing value assurance approach. Note the changing focus.

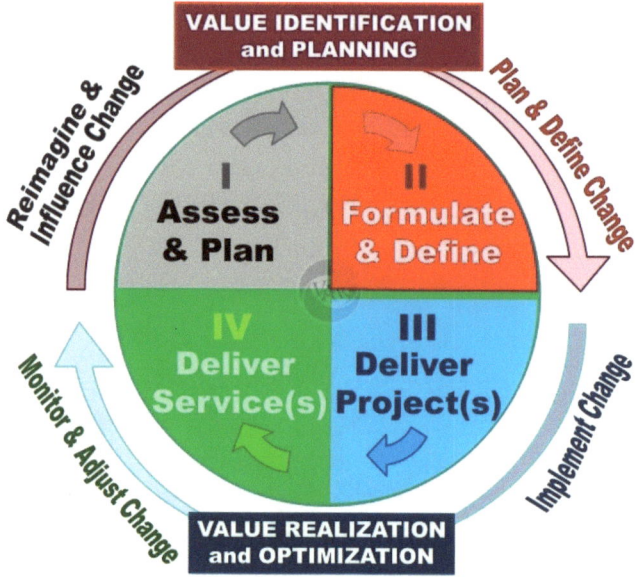

Figure C.   360° Application and Changing Focus

Reviews are conducted for the purposes of:

– **<u>Value Identification and Planning</u>**
  I. **Early Application at the Planning Stage**
  - to appraise overall requirements; establish strategic direction, optimal scoping and appropriate prioritization

  II. **Application During the Conceptualization Stage**
  - to formulate concept and select key systems and procedures; to fully define the project to be executed

❖ **<u>Value Realization and Optimization</u>**
  I. **Later Application to Resolve Emerging Problems During the Execution/Project Delivery Stage**
  - to avert or rectify budget and schedule overruns and other areas of deadlock

  II. **In-Service Program Turnaround / Optimization**
  - to optimize productivity / throughput and reduce unit operating costs.

Figure D illustrates the scope of application of value assurance for the management levels of (i) program oversight, and, (ii) program, as related to overall program/project progression.

Figure D. Scope of Value Assurance Application

❖ **Overall Program Oversight**
❖ **Project Level**

Note. Terminology may vary with jurisdiction.

Example value considerations for the aspects of both functionality and business are shown in **Figure E.**   In-depth information on value assurance may be obtained from the other *"Closing the Performance Gap"* series of publications listed on page 39.

Figure E. Example Project Value Considerations

1. Why This Guide?

Despite the mass of available processes, tools and techniques, many programs and major projects (including products, systems and services) fail to produce their expected performance. This can be due to a combination of ill-defined expectations, flawed planning and absence of appropriate controls, along with shifting managerial direction and waning stakeholder support. There is a general need for better coordination of the use of the various, accepted approaches to program, project, risk and value management.

Programs or projects can suffer from:
- Ambiguous requirements; approval delays, over design
- Changes of heart; scope creep; late delivery, under design
- Poorly defined deliverables; service disruption
- Surprises/unforeseen risks; poor value for money
- Lack of readiness to proceed to the next stage
- System defects; re-work; major claims; over-expenditure
- Frustrated staff, customers and other stakeholders
- Waning yields and increasing program expenses.

Similarly, organizations may exhibit difficulties such as:
- Multiple business goals - all being top priority
- Benefits yielded are much less than as forecast in the original business case
- Programs and projects that are delivered late, over-budget and not in line with the current business needs
- Reluctance to cancel non-performing programs or projects
- Over-abundance or misalignment of tools and techniques
- Over-stretched resources; consequent poor performance
- Organizational and "cultural" barriers
- Lack of innovation and drive (just "more of the same").

This booklet introduces an opportunity-based approach derived by integrating various management methods. Its purpose is to inspire a pro-active, holistic and systematic way of group thinking for driving best value, - through an end-to-end, and solidly anchored planning, delivery and assurance mechanism.

2.   Context

Organizations of all types and sizes rely on the successful implementation of project work to assist in achieving their business aims. Projects may be grouped within programs which in turn may fall under the umbrella of a portfolio. A major project in one organization may be larger than a portfolio of programs and projects in another organization. The term program may also refer to a service or series of activities that constitute provision of an operational service (rather than a project which has a defined start and finish). In this guide the term project also applies to products and systems. Key considerations for accomplishing successful programs and projects are listed on page 11.

The expression value encompasses a number of varying expectations that are not always just monetarily driven. Value and performance parameters are closely linked and wide ranging. Value may also be defined by the net benefit as related to the expenditure of resources required to derive that benefit. It would be reasonable to assume that portfolios, programs and projects are defined from the outset in terms of stakeholder requirements and related values and then evolved, monitored and adjusted accordingly. This would further assume that the portfolios, programs and projects are adequately resourced, planned and managed for the stated individual and group outcomes, without impinging on each other or causing negative collateral impacts (e.g. damage to third-party stakeholders or on future undertakings).

However, best value is often inadequately articulated and hence may appear somewhat elusive. For any portfolio, it is important that the following aspects are addressed in deciding which programs and projects should be allocated resources:
- Focus on strategically important outcomes
- Alignment of plans to business priorities and goals
- Robust management of program and projects for delivery of the expected value
- Adequate staffing, both in number and through training.

3. Creating the Conditions for Success

Most organizations depend on the accomplishment of projects as a source of service delivery, products, profits, or process improvements. To accomplish this, there is often a complex system of programs, priorities, policies, and practices that shapes the behaviors of managers and resources. This requires careful guidance and consistent coordination for maximum effectiveness. An environment of many projects can generate competing priorities for project resources and managers alike, and can make the requisite results difficult to achieve. There is great temptation for staff under budgetary and schedule pressures to circumvent exploratory, divergent thinking by converging too quickly on a set of solutions that has worked elsewhere.

Program and project quality, value for money, risk, cost-efficiencies and in-service performance are closely related and require strategic alignment, cross-linking, and continuing review. Clarity of focus and definition of the "vital few" influencing factors is essential, as is establishment of enduring performance criteria.

Major decisions are sometimes predicated on relatively flimsy criteria and projections. This can lead to the commitment of large sums of money and lengthy project development periods, during which time organizations are exposed to significantly changing conditions. True progress in programs and projects is often only evident at the "hand-offs" between resources, when the work completed by one resource allows another resource to start work. **Figure F** illustrates example elements of value assurance.

There must be "buy-in" to proposals to ensure that the resulting change delivers the anticipated results. Changing corporate direction can incur a great deal of time, money and perhaps resentment. Effort spent in developing unambiguous, acceptable strategic direction is undeniably a good investment. To guide sustaining decisions, participants should view the whole picture before focusing on specifics. From the outset there should be a framework for understanding what constitutes end-to-end program value, along with a system for managing risk and change.

Figure F. Example Value Assurance Elements

Note: Organizational efficiencies, scope, cost, schedule and quality control are implicit throughout the process.

These and other various activities may occur at other times or concurrently; some (e.g. consultation and risk management) may continue throughout. Note also that some organizations include Initiation, Planning, Execution, Monitoring & Controlling and Closing in every key stage of project management.

4. Assurance of Results

Due to shifting business dynamics, an organization's needs may change before full program development or project completion. Particularly in complex business environments, managers need to have a reference framework for ensuring confidence in program and project delivery to suit changes in circumstances or events. Decisions based on an understanding of the full cost of ownership or other life-cycle implications of an asset and services are to be encouraged. Assurance for stakeholders is required such that their portfolios and programs and projects remain viable in terms of:

- Business aims (benefits, scope and costs)
- User requirements (availability, serviceability) operability, reliability and compliance capabilities)
- Technical merit (feasibility and fitness-for-purpose)
- Supply chain capabilities and compatibilities
- Likelihood of meeting forecast targets.

Organizations go through cycles of change of staff, culture and program focus. In so doing, the organizations can lose their collective memory and expertise, thus sometimes having to learn again some fairly basic, corporate project management skills. Executives need reliable processes to ensure that their organization's current efforts and proposed changes are truly cost-effective and meet corporate objectives. It also ensures that the most appropriate aspects are addressed adequately and that best value is obtained within controlled risk parameters.

The key performance indicators (KPIs) for each level of the organization should be articulated in the simplest terms possible. The KPIs should be linked through each organizational level and target the particular aspects that influence the most important metrics of success (for example, customer satisfaction). Performance reporting against the KPIs should be as simple as appropriate to the level to which is being reported. A formal value file should be established at the outset of each program and project, and be maintained on a consistent basis throughout the life of the program or project, from inception to final disposition.

5. Program & Project Oversight

There is ever increasing scrutiny of program and project outcomes. Senior management and project boards, along with other key stakeholders, are seeking greater confidence that their project(s) will in fact perform financially, functionally and on-time, as promised. As part of the overall portfolio value assurance process, program and project oversight is established. This complements traditional project management systems through high level monitoring and reporting of progress. By being free of the daily issues and activities of the project management team, the assurance process can also provide insight into areas that may not have been fully considered. Particularly for sensitive and complex undertakings, this reinforces the team's efforts and ensures that progress is being made along the right track, thus contributing significantly to the confidence felt by stakeholders.

Independent, formal certification of proposals as good value for money is an additional benefit, especially to effectively engage additional resources and partners. In addition, performance assessment & reporting (see page 25) comprises objective, independent, review functions to confirm compliance with overarching, approved plans. The keys to success are to:

a) Set the appropriate tone from top management, ensuring clear accountabilities, alignment, awareness, training and support for assurance teams within the business unit(s)
b) Clarify the framework for the management of programs & projects and communicate procedures to all stakeholders
c) Allocate adequate time upfront to establish effective project planning, review and control systems, and develop /update a comprehensive program or project plan
d) Confirm a proper understanding of needs, clarity of purpose, lean team structure(s), clear roles, responsibilities and contractual arrangements for implementation
e) Embed a strong value and risk management culture, along with a partnering / incentive-based alliancing style
e) Ensure suitable readiness to proceed to each next stage.

6.   Why Use Value Assurance?

An abundance of management tools and techniques exists, yet many programs and projects do not perform to management's expectations. There is a tendency to utilize various improvement approaches as separate interventions, rather than as part of an integrated management planning and control plan. There can also be a significant variation in "organizational maturity" levels within and between organizations, which can complicate the mix of interactions and capabilities. A major challenge, particularly for large organizations, is in being able to demonstrate to shareholders and other stakeholders that best overall value / optimum performance is being provided. So often, project development and / or implementation teams are unaware of the overall value expected from their undertakings. For example:

- Business goal-setting persons and their performance criteria are often absent during project development
- Return on investment (R.O.I.) criteria are not clearly disseminated and therefore not necessarily attained
- Key knowledgeable people are lost to the next critical program or project; information may not be passed on and assumptions are then made by the next wave of staff
- Program service / yield no longer matches expectations.

Underlying concept(s) must be tested well, prior to program/project development. Otherwise the most efficiently implemented programs and projects can yield only limited value. A well-communicated, strategic framework is necessary for deriving balanced solutions to complex and divisive issues, also taking into account financial, legal, political, regulatory, schedule, resource and technical implications. A comprehensive, but easy to interpret, system of "cradle to grave" checks and balances is needed to maximize corporate performance and key supporting initiatives. Typically, implementation of a revised program of work or new project will necessitate some change. Projects which utilize value assurance and integrate change management as a part of their business change tend to be more successful and better received by those persons impacted by the change.

7. Project Management

Many organizations already have project management policies and procedures. Yet, some projects still cause surprises to senior management, with scope increases, cost overruns, schedule delays and general stakeholder dissatisfaction. How can this be?

Often there is a significant disconnect between senior and middle management regarding project expectations, true progress and processes or systems. Detailed administrative procedures abound, but are they cumbersome, not communicated well or just inappropriate for a particular application? Some project managers are so engaged in daily detail that they cannot keep up with the overall process requirements and especially the demanding steps and expectations of project approval.

Program and project woes are often built in from the start. Busy managers demand a quick estimate of cost and schedule that is inserted hastily in a budget document for future years' expenditure. These numbers remain the official parameters until the project meets its inevitable exposure to a severe overrun. Other managers, upon being given a high budget cost estimate, "massage" the number until it appears more acceptable to the approval authority. Ultimately the true implications emerge and the project image suffers accordingly; taking with it the reputation of the project staff involved. Accountabilities must be clearly defined and aligned with priorities.

Project management seeks to formalize, define and constrain that which can be quite fuzzy. Conflicting aims are:

a) users trying to retain flexibility of options, and

b) implementers requiring certainty of scope, data, schedule, cost, risk, etc.

Many different, formal project management systems have evolved over time or have been developed for specific organizations or application areas. A "one size fits all" approach is not recommended. Flexibility and clarity must be maintained.

8. Managing Uncertainty

An understanding of risk and formal ways to manage uncertainty is being seen increasingly as an essential part of smart business and project management. Risk management is applied at the levels of: enterprise, portfolio, program, and individual projects including critical systems & components.

Risk (both negative and positive) and uncertainty may arise internally or externally. Internal uncertainty may relate to business aims, scheduling, resourcing, etc. External uncertainty, which is usually more difficult to deal with, may relate to regulatory approvals, land acquisition, politics, environmental opposition, economic trends, etc. Risks may be present due to limited experience, lack of information and general uncertainty regarding future conditions and viewpoints. Risks may also occur as parties, personnel and relationships change during the course of a long duration project. In particular, inaccuracy of projections and other basic assumptions can lead to major areas of uncertainty. Project risk management should be concentrated particularly during the early planning and development stages. Combined risk and value studies can be particularly effective.

While neglect to identify a risk can be expensive, so can unnecessary allowance to avoid each and every possible risk that may be envisaged. Further, once identified, risk may be examined creatively and turned into a scheduling or economic opportunity. A balanced approach is advocated to identifying and specifying methods to address risks at different levels. There are several risk management protocols issued by various authoritative bodies globally. Some are quite prescriptive in nature, others are fairly general; the overall basic principles being as follows:

- Identification - determine what could go wrong
- Assessment - understand how the risks occur; quantify possible effects, mitigated versus unmitigated
- Management - the continuing process of registering and re-evaluating risks and reviewing options for reducing their potential effects.

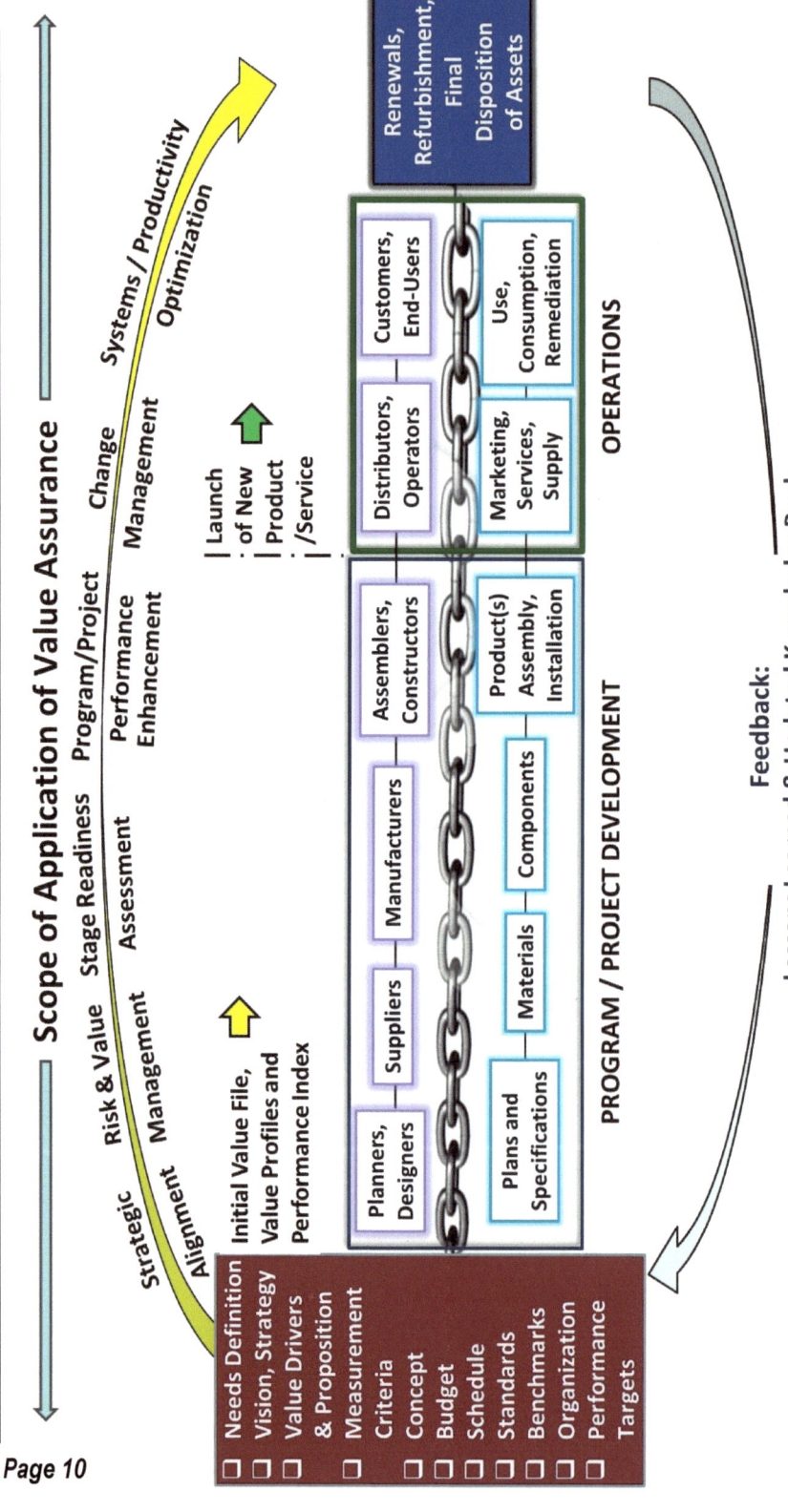

Scope of Application of Value Assurance

Figure G. Program / Project Value Chain

9. Key Factors for Success

Accomplishment of successful portfolios, programs and projects requires consideration of a number of factors including:

- ☐ Strategic alignment of plans, processes and resources
- ☐ Consideration of the "voice of the customer"
- ☐ Development and maintenance of stakeholder consensus
- ☐ Establishment of value metrics from the outset
- ☐ Innovative and sustainable solutions; societal commitment
- ☐ Focus on functional performance and benefits
- ☐ Explicit derivation of best value solutions
- ☐ Managed risk throughout development & operations
- ☐ Formal evaluation of readiness to proceed to each stage
- ☐ Resource competencies, readiness and utilization
- ☐ Continuing value improvement
- ☐ Change management assessment and implementation
- ☐ Assurance of results that match the original business plan
- ☐ Feedback of "lessons" learned to other programs & staff
- ☐ Transparency of decisions and clear support for the value assurance process from "the top" and throughout all levels of management & supervision
- ☐ Clear delineation of roles, responsibilities, authority and decision-making
- ☐ Client - customer relationships and trust
- ☐ Stakeholder consensus and conflict avoidance/resolution
- ☐ Processes scaled to complexity of program
- ☐ A managerial 'bias for action"
- ☐ Up-to-date specifications and willingness to innovate
- ☐ Active leadership, involvement of employees and partnership development; streamlined, but linked reports for each level
- ☐ Integrated application of management tools and techniques
- ☐ Decisions based on sound data & performance measurement.

Figure G shows various activities along the entire value chain.

10. Selection of Programs & Projects

Management of a portfolio should drive a path toward achieving stated strategic objectives and, ideally, the route of continuing improvement gains across the whole enterprise. Programs and projects should clearly support attainment of the corporate vision statement and principles.

While program and project selection is often made based on largely economic or financial terms, it has become extended to include aspects such as environmental friendliness and certainty of performance. In this regard value drivers (project characteristics that are most important to stakeholders) are critical to identify and apply. Use of "value drivers" brings issues into sharp focus. Strategies focused through value drivers bridge, or eliminate, the "performance gap" and guide the implementation of effective change programs. A value–focused, turnaround strategy addresses where value and performance are being inhibited or slipping away from the organization. A particular challenge exists when programs and projects are promoted and approved for purely political purposes, without being subjected to the rigors of a formal appraisal, selection, planning and resourcing process.

Tools for the selection and sorting of programs and projects include use of:

- Financial projections -net present value analysis, payback analysis, return on investment
- Multi-criteria profiling and performance /value index
- Needs prioritization.

Utilizing a combination of value and risk assessment enables comparison and prioritization of competing proposals, as well as formulation and management of the portfolio. Logically, an organization would give priority to the higher value programs and projects that have manageable risk. Timely assignment of adequate resources should be ensured.

11. Group Innovation

Innovation is said to be at the heart of corporate strategy and competitive advantage for many of the world's leading organizations. Unilateral decision-making is now relatively uncommon in progressive corporations. Today, decision by consensus is more the norm. This requires a suitable guiding process that will also encourage innovation and sustaining results.

Every project is unique in terms of conditions and constraints, stakeholders and their requirements, as well as timing and budgets. Performance improvement deals with a range of situations, complexities and philosophies. Inclusive, multi-functional, group problem-solving defines the most appropriate options, builds consensus and overcomes implementation hurdles quicker than the traditional routing back and forth between isolated departmental viewpoints.

Relationship building and group synergy are important ingredients in the formula for success. A major factor in the success of leading organizations is the use of participatory (i.e. group) problem solving to enable them to:

- Adapt to the external environment
- Continually enhance the capability to change/adapt
- Identify and develop innovative ideas
- Encourage individual and collective learning
- Use the results of such learning to achieve better results.

There are various forms of group problem-solving methods. However, most methods tend to be conducted as specific interventions, in isolation from one another and through different participants. It is far better to adopt an integrated approach to the use of such methods. It is particularly important to ensure accuracy and consistency of information, along with the "packaging" of outputs for submission to executive management.

12. Consensus Development

Decision-making for complex situations can be fraught with pitfalls if a logical and consultative framework is not used. Common problems with decisions are that they are formulated before all the facts are available, too narrowly based and unable to withstand the scrutiny of an audit. There may be multiple objectives and preferences to be aligned for a variety of stakeholder groups. As well, the groups may well have different attitudes toward the key decision criteria of cost, time, risk, return-on-investment, and socio-environmental aspects. Accordingly, as most situations are unique, it is crucial to understand the context and nature of the surrounding circumstances before arriving at any particular decision.

Change management efforts that fail are likely to be caused by poor relationships and / or lack of a change framework and follow-through. Consensus building and careful attention to both process and people aspects are becoming ever more necessary, along with formal change management. Multi-criteria decisions require careful treatment; this is where structured consensus building has particular application. The consensus building process has to be carefully designed and managed to suit the unique circumstances of various situations.

Consensus building offers a way for individuals and organizations to collaborate on solving complex problems in ways that are acceptable to all. Consensus building is a process that allows everyone on the team to contribute to determining the group's final recommendation. Consensus cannot be forced; it must be nurtured. Consensus-building takes time and effort and, for complex situations, is typically accomplished incrementally and through a number of iterations. The purpose is to make decisions with more confidence of appropriateness, stakeholder support and longevity of application. It is crucial to understand the context and ramifications of a far-reaching decision before implementing the changes. As well, a dispute or conflict resolution process should be in place.

13. Change Management

Change is now the norm and resistance (at all levels) can be immense. For those who seek to maintain the status quo, change is seldom seen to be in their own interest. By the same token, change may be seen as a great idea for other people to experience. There are generally four types of change: technology, products and service, human resources and administrative, each with their own considerations, impacts and interactions.

Most new initiatives and projects will lead to change. For the outcomes to be fully realized, the change must, typically, be carefully managed. Change may be effected through different approaches, ranging from a dictatorial directive through to a high degree of collaboration. For complex and sensitive situations of significant change affecting a wide diversity of stakeholder groups, it can be useful to treat the process of change management as a separate project in parallel with the technical project - each process with its own tools and techniques.

Effective change may well take longer to effect than expected. The schedule and communication plan should take into account a number of considerations and specific steps. This requires an estimation of the stakeholders' relative degree of readiness for, and commitment to, the proposed change(s). As with everything else in business and project management, a good communication plan is vital to:

- Keep stakeholders informed of proposals and progress
- Align the project/initiative with other initiatives
- Gauge the degree of support or resistance to the initiative
- Avoid misunderstandings and develop active support
- Enable stakeholders to allocate resources appropriately.

Process improvement disciplines that are purely engineering centric and problem-solving in nature tend to ignore change management, thereby experiencing a higher degree of employee resistance and difficulties during implementation.

14. Leadership Development

Effective leadership is required to bring about the expected outcomes of organizations, business programs and related projects. Leadership styles vary, as do the differing circumstances for their application; leaders should know when to exhibit a particular approach. Some recognized leadership styles are listed below:

- Authoritative - command and control
- Bureaucratic - by the book; hold the line
- Charismatic - inspirational
- Collegial - by example; persuasive
- Laissez-faire - hands-off.

Leadership may be defined as "getting people to do what you want them to do because they want to do it". With the exception of the bureaucratic style, leadership is all about change. Much has been debated about the differences between leadership and management for various situations and changing times. Managing a portfolio, large program of projects or mega project requires a quite different skill set and experiences from those for running most projects.

Leadership also requires "followership". It has been said that "great followers create great leaders and organizations". As well, the characteristics of a good follower can be those of a good leader; tomorrow's leaders may be drawn from today's followers. Even great leaders have to follow direction from others (e.g. a higher level leader or committee). Effective leadership in organizations is not always evident. Followers can look beyond a leadership void by having a strong commitment to the group or organization and its mission.

According to a former Speaker of the U.S. House of Representatives "*You cannot be a leader and ask other people to follow you unless you know how to follow too.*" Learning to be an effective follower can help develop critical leadership traits. With dynamic leader–follower interaction, it is more likely that suitable change management can be accomplished.

15. Organizational Aspects

Much has been espoused in other publications about overall organizational performance. Various surveys indicate that *(i) a high proportion (up to 40%) of payroll is spent on non-value adding items, (ii) major declines (as much as 30%) in shareholder value can be attributed to organizational project management capacity, supply chain inefficiencies and poor operational control.*

Currently, there is a lot of interest in "organizational excellence" (for which there are many definitions). According to Excellence Canada, "*Excellent organizations continually improve performance; they are innovative, competitive, and customer focused; they are healthy, inclusive, and sustainable; and they are economically, socially, and environmentally responsible*". Values relate to *people, relationships, integrity, dedication and excellence.*

Organizational efficiency tends to refer to the capacity of an organization to produce desired results with a minimum (or reducing) expenditure of resources. In contrast, organizational effectiveness usually measures the extent to which an organization derives certain outcomes (which may not always be quantifiable). It is worth reflecting on what the consequences would be for not building high performance practices into your organization. To nurture organizational excellence, leaders need to focus on aligning strategies, systems and capabilities as well as engaging their people and external stakeholders.

Key management areas and characteristics of successful organizations include attention to: governance, leadership, planning, customers, employees, work processes, systems thinking and delivery, performance measurement, suppliers & partners, resource management, communications, continuous improvement, societal commitment and emergency preparedness. Explicit consideration of best overall value, cash flow, risk management, readiness to proceed, realism of cost and scheduling estimates, along with quality management is critical. Application of value assurance brings together all of these factors and enhances organizational performance capabilities.

16. Application of VA

It may be said that, like beauty, value is in the eye of the beholder. Value may have many dimensions and varies according to one's position and circumstances. Multi-stakeholder situations tend to have quite complex value systems that can also vary over time.

The performance of programs, projects, products and services is inextricably linked with quality, value and risk. Despite the availability of an abundance of project management techniques and training, together with a plethora of professionals in most large organizations, many projects fail to satisfy all shareholders and users. There is often a missing link between the day-today administration of projects to satisfy institutionalized procedures and the objective, strategic thinking required to achieve best overall value and stellar performance for the corporation, stakeholders and external partners. Missed deadlines, mission/scope creep, overspent budgets, reduced functionality and operational "hiccups", together with shareholder dissatisfaction and other stakeholder concerns are all part of an unacceptable value gap. It is clearly inappropriate for management to deny the problem or to shuffle the problem off to the next phase of the project development and execution.

At its simplest, the value gap is measured by the difference between actual and optimal total cost and functionality. Typically, the value gap is caused by a performance gap which is often described in terms of excessive cost and time, reduced functionality and often requires rework. Consider a large design-build project that required significant cost reduction after the receipt of four pre-qualified bids. The owner wanted to cut costs by 30%, but application of typical cost cutting efforts yielded less than 10%. After a number of months of minor re-designs had elapsed, the functional, value-based thinking approach was applied to the project and this led to a breakthrough of 35% in total project cost savings, quicker implementation, less environmental & social disruption, plus significantly enhanced, long-term functionality. Other such examples are not uncommon.

16. Application of VA (Cont.d)

Clearly, procedures are necessary to ensure that best value for the organization is identified and not allowed to be lost. A comprehensive, but easy to interpret, system of "cradle to grave" checks and balances is required to maximize corporate performance. Thinking outside their comfort zones requires people to be receptive to new ideas and to those of others. This calls for broader and less defensive thinking, such that the end result is not merely "more of the same". Re-skilling of organizations and individuals may be necessary to produce the dramatic improvements in value that major corporations are demanding. A thorough understanding of the value chain (or value stream) and functional requirements is necessary.

VA pertains to deriving, maintaining and confirming best overall value, along with managed risk, for portfolios, programs and individual projects. VA also provides a means to communicate regularly to executive management and stakeholders that portfolios, programs and projects will realistically:

a) yield best value and return-on-investment

b) deliver within the specified timeframe & allocated budget

c) be adjusted, as necessary, to suit changing conditions.

VA encourages collaborative, performance-driven working and is applied over the whole program / project life. It ensures that the expectations or results gap between management levels is closed, and that commitments are followed through. Use of VA simplifies the processes for multi-level reporting and key decision-making, thus allowing project staff to focus on their day-to-day duties. A suitably experienced and well-rounded VA coordinator (internal or external) reports directly to executive management on a regular basis.

The formal value assurance process works in parallel to the day-to-day program and project delivery activities. The VA levels (illustrated in **Figure B,** page vii) comprise: 1. executive oversight (*value assurance*); 2. coordination of performance reviews, value enhancements and overview reporting (*performance assurance*); 3. value & risk management studies/interventions.

An Introduction to Value Assurance

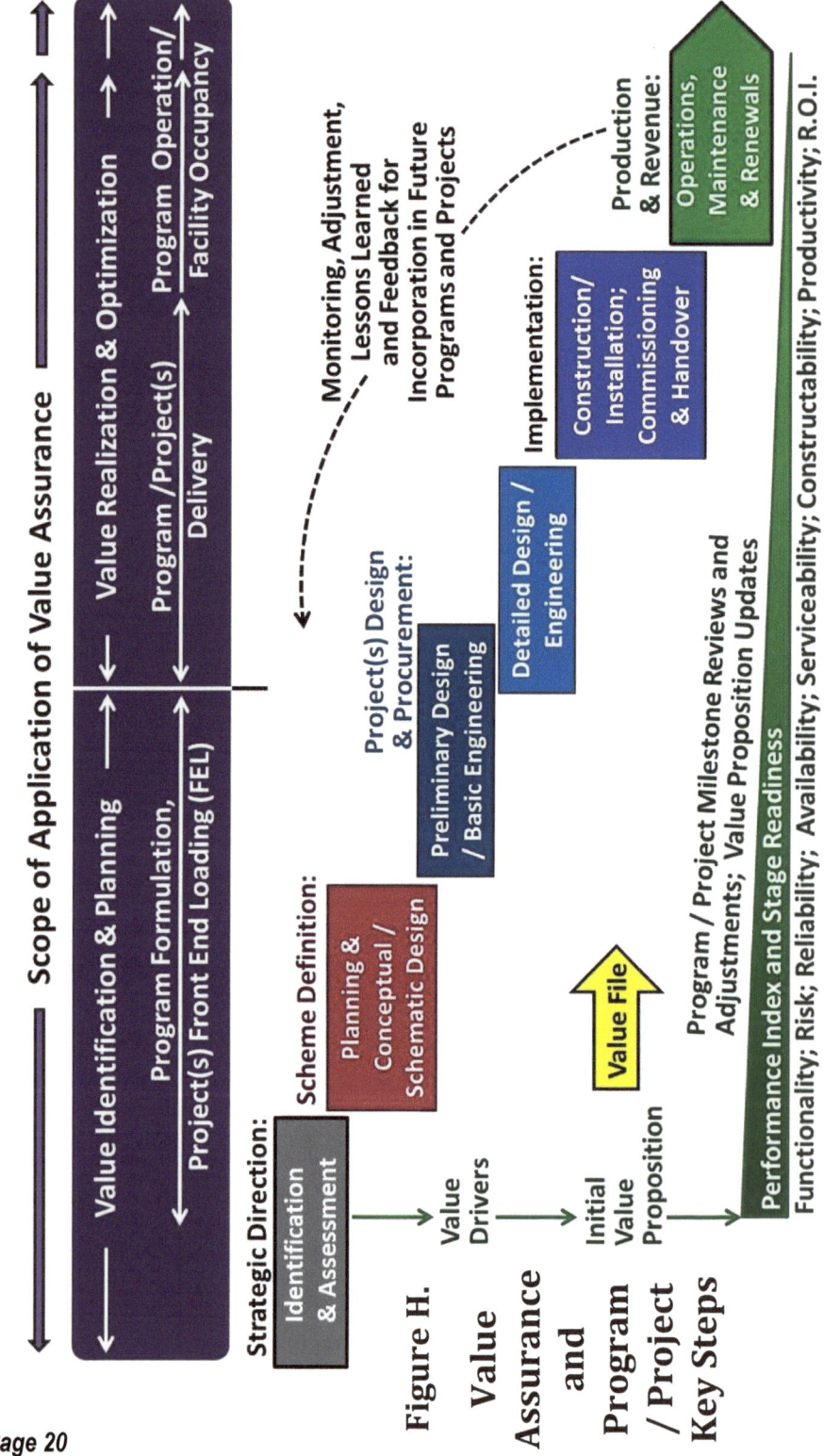

Figure H. Value Assurance and Program / Project Key Steps

16. Application of VA (Cont.d)

Value assurance starts as early as needs analysis, development of the service delivery model and formation of alliances. VA tasks extend across a broad range of activities and timescales, from strategic alignment of stakeholder expectations and business plans, through confirming the best overall fit of developing program/project proposals, to optimizing an in-service system or facility. The key steps and scope of application of value assurance are illustrated in **Figure H**. The VA process is results -oriented and is scalable for programs and projects of various sizes and complexity. In essence, VA provides a:

- Strategic navigation aid for best value programs & projects
- Stakeholder consensus building aid for complex situations
- Set of program analytical and remedial tools & techniques
- Continuing "health check" for reviewing program and critical project capabilities for meeting stakeholder needs.

The fundamentals of the two-part VA oversight process (for a range of contractual arrangements) are:

1. **Strategic Value Planning** through *Value Assurance Reviews (VAR)*. Consensus building on issues & options for resolution of complex situations. Program turnaround and project realignment. Establishment of key decision points & criteria.

2. **Performance Monitoring and Value Enhancement** through *Performance Assessment & Reporting (PAR)*. Milestone reviews to diagnose, report and adjust from definition through development and execution to operation. Performance improvement during delivery of programs and projects previously not meeting business expectations. Cost savings, functionality enhancements & schedule optimization

The all-important value file is established early and continuously maintained on a consistent basis for the life of the program or project. The key features of the value file are:

- Vital statistics for attaining required performance
- Key performance requirements and decision points
- Record of key decisions and variances
- Smart links to various other management levels.

17. Value Improvement Methods

An unchallenged "first thought' concept, or the single-solution fixation (e.g. what worked well previously), can prove to be very costly and lead to a significant value gap. Most value / performance enhancement gains are made through strategic analysis and in conjunction with stakeholder input. However there are typically other downstream opportunities to add more value, or conduct course corrections, as a program or project proceeds through development to implementation and routine operation.

Value analysis (sometimes referred to as value engineering) is the *application of a systematic exploration of a program, project, product, system, or facility to understand current or designed functionality and performance for the purpose of identifying potential areas for improvement.*

Value engineering (according to US Public Law 104-106) is *"an analysis of the functions of a program, project, system, product, item of equipment, building, facility, service, or supply of an executive agency, performed by qualified agency or contractor personnel, directed at improving performance, reliability, quality, safety, and life cycle costs".*

Value management (according to the UK Institute of Value Management) is *"based on principles of defining and adding measurable value, focusing on objectives before solutions, and concentrating on function to enhance innovation. It uniquely combines within an integrated framework a value focused management style; a positive approach to individual and team motivation; an awareness of the organisational environment; and the effective use of proven methods and tools."*

Value improving practices (VIPs) are utilized in the petrochemicals processing industry in particular. Value engineering (often conducted in an abbreviated form) is just one of 17 VIPs, which are typically applied over a very short timeframe. VIPs are required typically to be unique, documented, optional and not part of everyday management tools.

18. Value Methodology

The value methodology (VM) is the formal process used to conduct value analysis/engineering/management studies. The VM objectively challenges assumptions, identifies alternative options, prioritizes according to agreed criteria and then develops and tests the proposed action plan for practicality of implementation. It is a very powerful, "fast-tracking", consensus development tool. Innovation is at its core.

The methodology is unique in the way it analyzes by function and integrates all aspects of a project, product, process or service. Analysis by function and functional dependencies is very powerful. It is the crux of a successful value study and differentiates the value-based approach from other management philosophies and tools. A principle of VM, as originally conceived as value analysis in the 1940s, is to maximize value by providing functionality and quality at the lowest cost. VM is also used in target cost management and new product development. More than a single application of the VM may be required as product or project development proceeds.

All VM study participants need to have a similar appreciation of the various stakeholders' values and constraints. A value workshop process facilitates this to take place, together with providing a step-by-step methodology for exploring various options to arrive at the most suitable solution. The VM workshop process is central to any formal value engineering or management study. The workshop is preceded by a number of preparatory and follow-up activities. Consensus on options is a key outcome.

Workshop teams are multi-disciplinary and represent the interests of all groups who may be impacted by the project under consideration. The mix of team members varies with the stage that the project is at, and whether an integrated team or an external, third-party team is used. The value methodology delivers remarkable results in a short timeframe. Adequate follow-through activities are essential for the expected value improvement to be realized and maintained in practice.

19. Strategic Performance Alignment

The key to aligning performance is through recognition and appropriate attention of stakeholder perspectives and values. Strategic Performance Alignment (SPA) is a "front-end" process that embodies the principles of the value methodology and risk management.

Most value enhancement gains are made through strategic decisions and in conjunction with stakeholder input. This typically involves the pro-active management of several interfaces and complex relationships. It is becoming universally accepted that tomorrow's high performing organizations will be those that utilize the problem-solving and decision-making capabilities of their entire teams.

SPA develops a framework for deriving balanced solutions to complex and divisive issues, taking into account also financial, legal, political, regulatory, schedule, resource and technical implications. This is accomplished through refocusing business programs and resources; - by proper identification and understanding of the issues, stakeholder values and strategic intent at an early stage, together with involvement and clear focusing of the appropriate team members at the right times.

The various steps involve an iterative process of issues identification, development of a vision, principles, strategic action areas, strategies, initiatives, target levels of service and indicators for success. This includes testing the rationale, functionality, life cycle impacts, relative cost-benefit, affordability and acceptability to all stakeholders. Significant attention must be paid to proper definition and adequate description of the success criteria, which translate into project performance / evaluation criteria. It is ultimately conformance to these criteria that determines interim approvals and overall success. As well, the value spiraling technique (VST) - see book 4 listed on page 39 - is a powerful process to establish strategic direction among many stakeholder groups and to then progress to program and project specifics.

20. Performance Assurance

Some project management systems may seem cumbersome to use in practice. Many program and project managers still appear to trust their instincts in the management of everyday work rather than use established tools to verify interim results. As such, for example, risks and their potential mitigation may not be identified until too late. Consequently, projects may be delayed, exceed approved budget or suffer from quality problems. Aside from the direct impacts, this will likely have adverse effects on other areas, projects, programs or stakeholders' cash flow; shareholder value will ultimately suffer accordingly.

Figure J illustrates that for consistently high performing outcomes, it is necessary to ensure both good value concepts <u>and</u> efficient execution/delivery. As a sub-set of the value assurance framework ***performance assurance,*** through performance assessment & reporting (PAR), provides an oversight and verification function, reporting on compliance with approvals. PAR bridges the awkward communication gap between middle and senior management. PAR works in parallel with the leading project management standards and focuses on compliance with the overarching intent and approved plans for programs, projects and cross-cutting initiatives that stretch across organizational boundaries. While value assurance pertains to deriving best overall value and managed risk for portfolios, programs and individual projects, performance assurance implements a verification function and highlights remedial requirements.

PAR is applied at the levels of both program and individual projects. It provides funders and other key stakeholders with confidence that, for a defined scope, deliverables will be on time, within approved budget and of acceptable quality. This is accomplished through a framework that provides independent oversight and coordinates gateway (or milestone) monitoring reviews along with objective assessment reporting, - conducted by appropriately skilled and experienced assurance personnel.

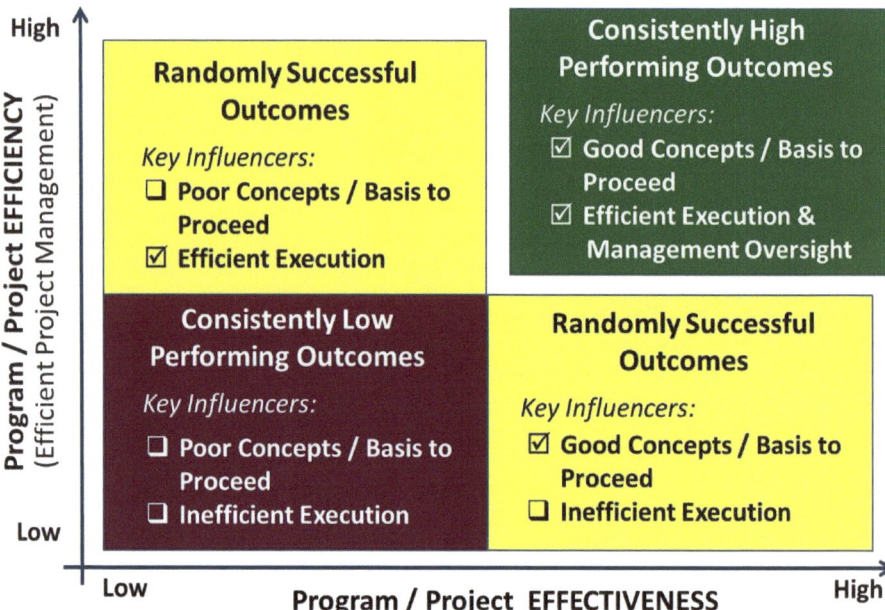

Figure J. Efficiency Vs. Effectiveness

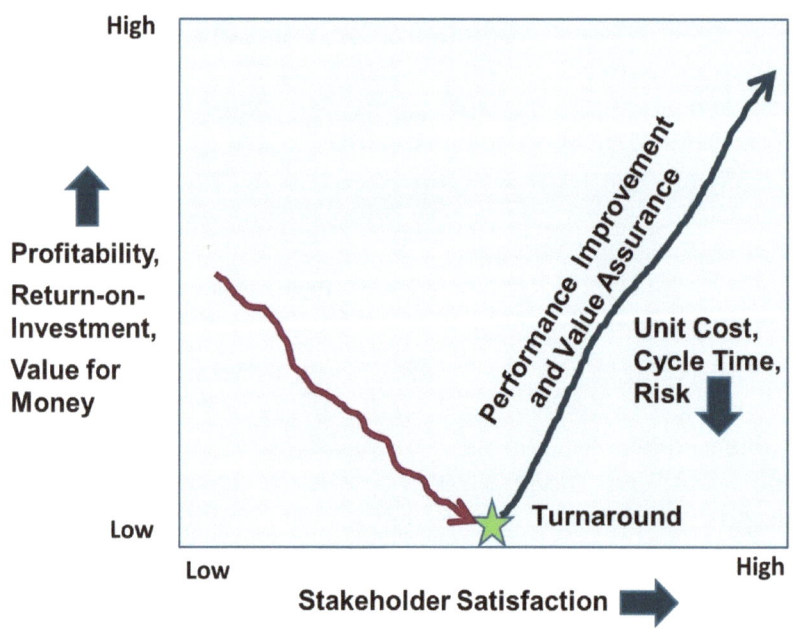

Figure K. Program Turnaround

21. Value Search

The Value Search® (VS) approach provides an effective framework and toolset to conduct value assurance and its sub-set, performance assessment and (overview) reporting. It is a broadly based, business turnaround and assurance process that maximizes team performance and program effectiveness. Through structure and innovation, VS is a multi-stakeholder process ensure attainment of best value/performance and return on investment.

VS is directed particularly at balancing the inputs and outputs, along with life cycle requirements, for programs, projects, products, systems, services, major strategies and complex situations. It is particularly useful for building consensus to identify, model, test, develop and prove innovative concepts prior to approval to proceed further with commitment of significant resources. VS is applied across the full range of the business cycle for maximizing performance:

- Program oversight and turnaround (see **Figure K**)
- Strategic planning (to optimize a portfolio; develop a business case and master plan)
- Program development (for the most appropriate concepts to reach goals to deliver a program of improved services)
- Project execution (design enhancement, procurement optimization, construction acceleration & project rescue)
- Systems optimization (productivity gains and benefit-cost enhancement for in-service processes/systems).

In particular, VS includes a suite of specific processes, tools and techniques for: (i) owners' overall planning and control, (ii) designers and contractors, to enhance performance across the supply chain activities for significant undertakings. In this way, a number of common problems such as mid-program/project design changes that create delays, new work, obsolete work, and out-of-sequence work are pre-empted.

Value Search is applied as a continuing process at key milestones and decision points during the stages of: a) Strategic Direction; b) Scheme Definition; c) Project(s) Design and

21. **Value Search** (Cont.d)

Procurement; d) Implementation; e) Routine Operation, Maintenance, Renewals and Refurbishment; f) Monitoring and Adjustment. See **Figure H** (page 20) and also **Figure L** (page 29).

Value Search encourages a collaborative, partnering approach between key stakeholder organizations, project management and uses an array of techniques for value preservation and continuing performance improvement. It is an agile process that can be tailored to suit the unique circumstances of a particular applications and clients. *Value Search* adjusts to the natural rhythm of organizations and their program/projects planning, development and implementation process.

Examples of the *Value Search* toolset & outcomes include:
- Strategic diagnosis and performance review; benchmarks
- Strategic performance alignment and "design-to-cost"
- Risk assessment and mitigation aspects
- Readiness assessment to proceed to next stage
- Lifecycle cost and functionality improvement
- Performance diagnostic and value index
- Alliancing and innovation workshops
- Streamlined processes and leverage of staff resources
- Smart templates and information summary "roll-ups" with the ability to interrogate through different fields and examine various "what if" scenarios
- Consistency of approach; reduced approval times
- Change management assessment & implementation plan
- Enabling of key approvals & stakeholder endorsements
- Updated value file and auditable trail as the basis of key decisions and changes; certification of best value
- Program & project performance assessment protocol for ensuring on time, quality outcomes, within budget
- Automated executive style reporting linked to key measurement parameters at various management levels
- Optimization of service delivery.

Four key points of application for a long-term VA oversight program are illustrated in **Figure L**. Two review stages are during the *value identification and planning* part of the overall cycle. Two further review stages are during the following *value realization & optimization* part of the cycle. Review stage **I** **appraises** the performance of established operating system(s) and **identifies** parameters & potential projects for strategic improvement. Review stage **II** examines the initial formulation of a program or project and **evaluates** & **selects** the new concept. Review stage **III** focuses on the proposals for **definition** & **execution**. Review stage **IV** analyzes the **operation** of installed system(s) for effective performance in line with the original business case and subsequently changed conditions.

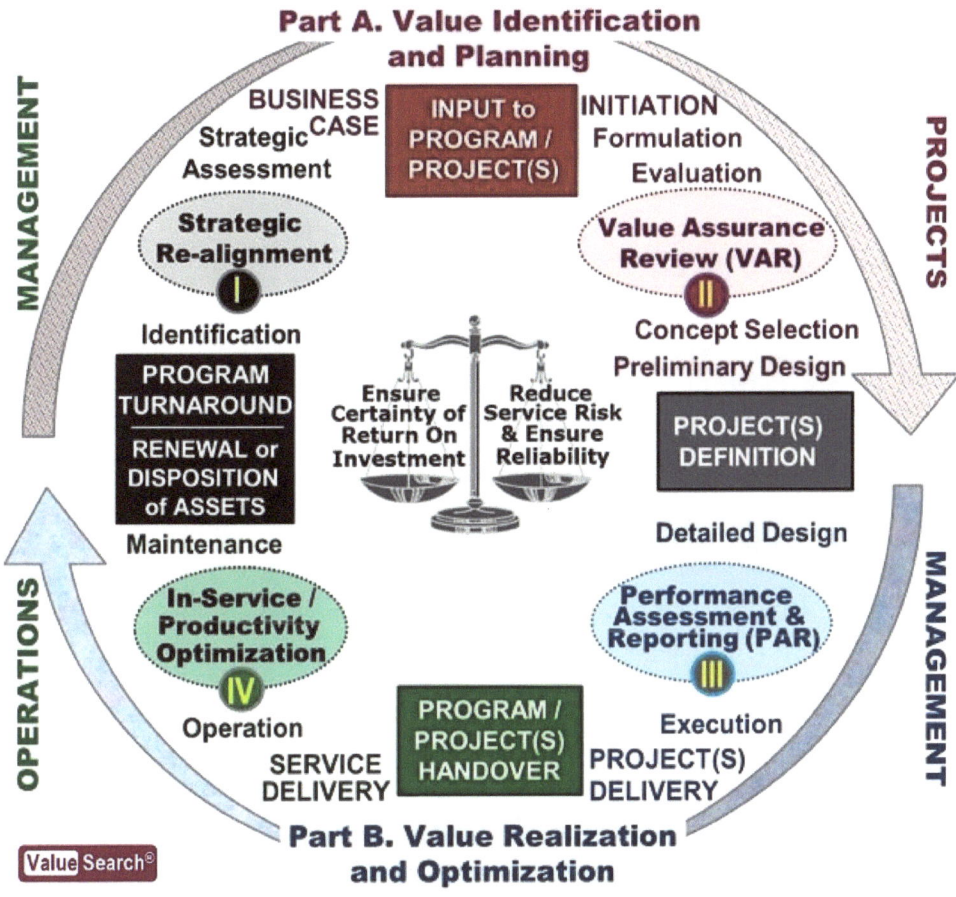

Figure L. Value Search Program Review Points

The *Value Search* framework is concerned with the whole (360 degrees) of a program's or project's life cycle, rather than just the capital development and execution process. The focus of each review stage varies as follows:

Stage I. Strategic Assessment / Alignment/Re-alignment.
Strategic Diagnosis – how well is the existing system meeting stakeholder needs and how capable is it of meeting future needs? **Identification** – are the implications of starting this new endeavor fully understood and addressed? What are the specifics of the stakeholder needs, problem definition & design requirements?

Stage II. Value Assurance Review (VAR). How can the program or project best meet the stakeholder requirements and criteria for success? **Evaluation** – have all the scenarios and corresponding options been considered and compared? Is the forecast item achievable technically and financially, taking into account other factors such as environmental and social considerations? **Concept Selection** – has the optimum choice of concept been made in view of all the requirements, constraints and related consequences? What are the special considerations to be taken into account during the subsequent phases?

Stage III. Performance Assessment & Reporting (PAR). Is the updated forecast for the project still in compliance with the business & functionality/quality success criteria? Resolve project deadlock. Is the project <u>fully</u> defined - through Preliminary Design and Detailed Design – and ready for Execution – while meeting all requirements & established value parameters? **Execution** – is the installation, construction or production and ultimately the delivery of a completed product in compliance with the Detailed Design Documents and execution Contract(s).

Stage IV. In-Service Productivity Review. Through a **Post Occupancy / Implementation Evaluation** and longer term **Optimization Review(s)**, how well were the decisions made and incorporated? Do the delivered outcomes still meet the forecast outcomes, stakeholder requirements and success criteria? What changes should be made for future endeavors?

Table 1 describes example key aspects of Value Assurance reviews for **Part A, *Value Identification and Planning*. Table 2** describes example key aspects of Value Assurance reviews for **Part B, *Value Realization and Optimization*.**

Stage	Part A Review Focus	Example Elements
Strategic Alignment/ Re-alignment of Program or Project(s) **Business Refocusing** **Program Turnaround** **Renewal or Disposition of Assets** **Appraisal (of existing) & Identification (of new) Programs and Projects**	**I. Value Assurance Review - Strategic Assessment** Consensus development on stakeholders' key issues. Agreed stakeholder needs and priorities Utilization of existing assets. Optimum value and affordability for customer /stakeholders. Assessment of current & predicted performance to requirements. Implications of change or no change. Unambiguous and tested business strategies and criteria. Business risks identification and mitigation strategy.	❖ **Situational Analysis** ❑ Strategic FOCUS diagram ❑ Cost, performance indices ❑ Needs evaluation. ❑ Benchmarking ❑ Internal/ external factors ❑ Interactions & unfolding circumstances ❑ Vision, principles, target service levels & scenarios. ❖ **Strategic Direction** ❑ Initial scoping & concept ❑ Testing & prioritization ❑ Strategic risk review ❑ Outline business plan ❑ Implementation & contract strategy ❑ Key performance indicators (KPIs) ❑ Value proposition ❑ **Identification** of preferred program / project(s) elements.
Front-End Formulation **Project Evaluation & Concept Selection** Value Search®	**II. Value Assurance Review - Formulation & Definition** Formulation and review of options to meet stakeholder requirements. Comparison of alternative concepts. Confirmation of best value program. Scope definition, performance parameters, key milestones and critical timelines. Risk & opportunity review.	▪ Value assurance plan ▪ Function analysis ▪ Cost / worth analysis ▪ Value drivers & criteria ▪ Performance profiles and value index ▪ Key risks evaluation ▪ Readiness index ▪ **Innovation Workshop** ▪ Recommendations & consultation ▪ Cost control framework ▪ Change management plan ▪ Monitoring parameters ▪ Initial value file.

Table 1. Value Identification & Planning

Stage	Part B Review Focus	Example Elements
Design, Development **Project Definition, Execution and Delivery**	**III. Performance Assessment and Reporting** **- Execution & Delivery** Verification of project requirements and capability to perform as specified. Consensus and confirmation of best value outline design, phasing and strategies. Implementation/force fitting of an "over-budget" project. Risk review & mitigation. Scheduling improvement.	❖ **Optimization Review** ❖ **Updates re.** ❑ Compliance with KPIs ❑ Function analysis ❑ Cost / worth analysis ❑ Value drivers and evaluation criteria ❑ KPIs, performance profiles and value index ❑ Key risks evaluation ❑ Readiness index ❑ Recommendations ❑ Stakeholder Consultation ❑ Change management Plan ❑ Monitoring parameters ❑ Value file.
Service Delivery **Service/ Systems Optimization** **Productivity Improvement** **Operational Analysis (including maintenance & renewals)** Value Search®	**IV. Performance Assessment and Reporting** **- In Service Optimization** Demonstration to higher management and stakeholders that anticipated business returns are being obtained. Resolution of emerging program or project significant efficiency, value or risk problems /opportunities. Recommendations for improvement or for future consideration. Attention to stakeholder concerns /satisfaction.	❖ **Critical Review** and improvement of in-service performance: ❑ Cost efficiency and operational effectiveness ❑ Conformance with predicted value parameters ❑ Risk & opportunity issues. ❖ **Value Analysis** to identify and evaluate potential options for improving operational efficiency and/or cost effectiveness. ❖ **Completion of feedback loop** to strategic planning process as part of the overall "expert" system and continuous improvement.

Table 2. Value Realization and Optimization

22. Summing Up

Programs and major projects need to reside within a clearly understandable, organizational framework that defines expectations and identifies and enforces key accountabilities. This requires a systematic approach to performance definition and improvement through a process of establishing strategic performance objectives, measuring performance, compiling analyzing and reporting performance data; - all with a view to addressing variances from targets and driving overall performance improvement. This also requires a system of linked performance objectives and indicators from the executive management level through to the performing level.

There are many and diverse aspects to be considered in the management of portfolios, programs and projects, e.g.:

- Governance and organizational effectiveness
- Strategic alignment & business case accuracy
- "Triple bottom line" of economics, community & environment
- Needs assessment and life cycle impacts
- Outcomes & benefits management
- Prioritization and authorization
- Policy setting & updates; service levels
- Specification & standards updates and approvals
- Options & value assessment
- Value improving practices
- Functionality, availability, serviceability and reliability
- Cost-effectiveness and affordability; equity with others
- Uncertainty and risk management
- Stage readiness to advance further and approvals
- Stage boundaries and interfaces
- Contracts strategy & management
- Resource management & partnerships
- Work processes, procedures and activities
- Performance measurement and continuous improvement processes & procedures

- Stakeholder consultation & issues management
- Change management strategy & conflict resolution
- Program and project managerial oversight
- Recognized project management processes: initiation, planning, execution, monitoring and controlling
- Recognized knowledge areas for management of projects: integration, scope, time, cost, quality, human resources, communications, risk, procurement, stakeholders, change control.

Inadequate consideration of any of these and/or other key aspects (as appropriate to a particular situation) will lead inevitably to some degree of loss of value to the organization or stakeholder(s). Comprehensive checklists and selected templates for different types of applications will be found in the companion publications.

With the plethora of readily available detailed "how to" procedures for so many tasks, it would otherwise be easy to be immersed in relative trivia and lose sight of the main goal and performance requirements.   The essence of the VA approach is to establish comprehensive value parameters, periodically measure aspects of the program against these parameters and then maintain or improve performance accordingly, throughout the entire life cycle.   VA drives conceptualizing, development and implementation of effective programs and projects, particularly by identifying and closing the performance/value gap and streamlining execution and reporting procedures.

Value assurance is a long-term, holistic process that is conducted through a series of interconnected events, the results of which influence corporate thinking and direction. By seeing the whole picture, value assurance has the ability to create powerful insights and steer undertakings toward better solutions in less time, with the optimal use of resources. The value assurance process is ideal for uncovering non-functional elements, driving out waste and responding to changing circumstances.   It guides, and ensures that, developing solutions are appropriate and up-to-date for the needs of the portfolio, program, project, product, service or system.

The value assurance process provides for **consistently high performing outcomes** re.

- Optimized concept, schedule and basis to proceed
- Continually tested solutions for long-term viability
- Continuously optimized in-service process or systems and feedback to the corporate data bank
- Recapture of (otherwise) lost value.

The VA process provides a framework and toolset to:

- Derive, confirm and maintain best overall value
- Certify suitability for funding approval(s)
- Ensure balanced solutions and is applicable to both "hard" and "soft" types of endeavours
- Conduct program and project turnaround
- Confirm accountabilities and provide transparency.

VA is an overarching, scalable system for:

- Owners to exercise strategic planning and control
- Designers and contractors to enhance performance across the supply chain for significant undertakings
- Integrating best management practices
- Applying checks and balances consistently
- Adjusting to changing circumstances
- *Closing the performance/value gap* between attainable and actual results
- Communicating critical data to executive management.

VA provides assurance to stakeholders that portfolios, programs and projects are, and remain, viable in terms of various expectations such as:

- Business aims (benefits, return-on-investment, scope and costs)
- User requirements (availability, serviceability, operability, reliability and compliance capabilities)
- Technical merit (comparative feasibility and fitness-for-purpose)
- Supply chain capabilities and compatibilities
- Meeting forecast targets.

About the Authors

Martyn Phillips, CVS®, CVM, FICE, FCIWEM, FHKIVM, FSAVE, P.Eng. PVM

Certified Value Specialist –Life (US); Certificated Value Manager (UK); Fellow, Institution of Civil Engineers (UK); Fellow, Chartered Institution of Water and Environmental Management (UK); Fellow, Hong Kong Institute of Value Management; Fellow, SAVE International (US); Professional Engineer (Canada), Professional in Value Management (EU)

Martyn Phillips is a seasoned value specialist with a strong background in both technical and project management. He has worked in several different countries and diverse cultures throughout the world. His leadership of opportunity and problem-solving explorations has resulted in substantial savings of time and capital (& life-cycle) cost.

This includes reduced risk and significant constructability / functionality / productivity enhancements, for many high profile, public and private sector programs, projects and services.

He is qualified as both an Engineer and a Value Specialist in Europe and in North America. He assists organizations achieve their business goals, particularly through planning & optimization of major initiatives. He is a Director of the Team Focus Group and is based in Alberta, Canada.

Martyn also conducts strategic and operational consulting assignments, as well as performance improvement training / coaching and change management for a wide range of clients and topics worldwide. His business activities also include organizational efficiencies and effectiveness, interim management, independent reviews, program / project planning and controls, as well as project rescue, along with transformation of business processes.

Shamsi B. Shishevan, MA, PMP, PMI-RMP

Master of Arts, Project Management Professional, Risk Management Professional

Shamsi Shishevan is a project, risk and value management consultant who has been involved in research, project planning, development, execution, controls and training. Fields of practice have included construction, manufacturing, petrochemicals and public service. She is familiar with the working cultures of Europe, the Middle-East and North America.

Her particular interests are strategic management, business process improvement, project/risk management process integration, value assurance, life cycle impact assessment & whole life cost improvement, training & development, stakeholder consultation and overall coordination for complex situations.

Fields of practice have included construction, manufacturing, petrochemicals and public service. She is experienced in the design and implementation of quality management systems for various manufacturing companies for sustainable process improvement programs. She has also managed ISO auditing and implementation of other quality management systems based on ISO 9001 ISO 9002(94), ISO 14001, QS9000, etc.

Shamsi has been practicing in the field of value and risk management since 2002. She has wide experience of group training for project, risk and value management, as well as coordination of a number of improvement studies for major projects. She is a Director of the Team Focus Group and is based in Alberta, Canada.

Publications in This Series

"Closing the Performance Gap" Series on Achieving Best Value Programs, Projects, Products, Systems & Services:

Executive Focus

In Search of Value
Aligning the Road to High Performance

1. **An Introduction to Value Assurance**
ISBN 978-1480011953

2. **Overview, Closing the Performance Gap with Value Assurance** ISBN 978-1477553831

Beginner* & Practitioner Focus

3. **Part 1, Managing Expectations: Understanding the Conditions for Success** ISBN 978-1468168150

4. **Part 2, Methods: Assuring Best Value and Managing Uncertainty** ISBN 978-1468168198

Value Solutions
Creating and Delivering Better Solutions in Less Time

5. **An Introduction to Conducting Value Studies** *
ISBN 978-0991737864

6. **Value Engineering Essentials** *
ISBN 978-0991737895

7. **Volume I, Value Methodology Fundamentals***
Basic Value Methodology "How To" Guide
ISBN 978-1477581032

8. **Volume II, Managing Value Management**
Intermediate VM Training Guide
ISBN 978-1477673751

Further information may be obtained from: info@valueassurance.org

You never change things by fighting the existing reality.

To change something, build a new model that makes the

existing model obsolete

**Source: R. Buckminster Fuller, American architect,
systems theorist, author, designer and inventor.**

www.ingramcontent.com/pod-product-compliance
Lightning Source LLC
Chambersburg PA
CBHW041110180526
45172CB00001B/184